Readings *for* Weddings

D1575005

For Nick
'That's how it is'

Readings
for Weddings

With a new Introduction

Compiled by
MARK OAKLEY

First published in Great Britain in 2004

Society for Promoting Christian Knowledge
36 Causton Street
London SW1P 4ST
www.spckpublishing.co.uk

Reprinted twice
Reissued 2013

Copyright © Mark Oakley 2004
New introduction copyright © Mark Oakley 2013

All rights reserved. No part of this book may be reproduced
or transmitted in any form or by any means, electronic or
mechanical, including photocopying, recording, or by any
information storage and retrieval system, without
permission in writing from the publisher.

SPCK does not necessarily endorse the individual
views contained in its publications.

British Library Cataloguing-in-Publication Data
A catalogue record for this book is available from the
British Library

ISBN 978-0-281-07095-4

Typeset by Pioneer Associates, Perthshire
Printed in Great Britain by Ashford Colour Press
Subsequently digitally printed in Great Britain

Produced on paper from sustainable forests

Contents

Poems and Reflections

Hymns

Introduction

A poem is like a stone thrown into a pool. There is an initial splash of words, and then the ripples slowly but relentlessly make their way towards your shore, shifting your sands slowly and creatively. This personal anthology does not attempt to be a comprehensive collection of the many readings that are suitable for every marriage service. It is, rather, a collection of poetic texts from the Jewish and Christian Scriptures, hymn writers and contemporary poets of different beliefs, whose ripples I have felt lap over me with both pleasure and surprise. The texts have not been forced into artificial pens but are free range, creating a book that can be dipped into by those wondering which words might best give some voice to what they are about to celebrate in their lives. As time has passed, there are many others I have encountered that I would like to be here, not least James Fenton's *Hinterhof* and Alice Oswald's *Wedding*, but every anthology has to end somewhere.

As I write, marriage is a very topical subject. Much debate takes place as to its nature and purpose and whether same-sex couples can enjoy its benefits. I am very clear that this book is for all couples who love each other, and who want to celebrate that love in a public act of commitment, with witnesses and those who are dear to them looking on and promising to be there for them as the years pass. Where mutual love is, God is. It is as simple, beautiful and miraculous as that.

I imagine that many people drawn to a book like this will be planning a wedding in a church. Personally, I think marriage services are best with two readings. The first might well be biblical and read before the address. The second can then be read after the vows have been taken and the initial blessing given, as a reflective or fun contribution to celebrate what has just taken place. Quite a few of the poems in this collection are humorous, because I believe humour is a promise of redemption, and faith is the intuition that the promise is being kept. The two go well together.

Towards the end of this collection are hymns which might be sung at a Christian marriage service. I hope that, by seeing these in an anthology of this type, we will be reminded of the poetry of faith that has shaped prayer and praise in good times and bad through many centuries. The hymns still have a marvellous way of praising the divine and bringing people together in one.

The readings from the Bible are from the New Revised Standard Version, except for the Psalms which I have taken from the Book of Common Prayer and the two readings from Tobit which are from the New American Bible. I hope, however, that couples will explore the various translations of the texts that are available.

I hope that clergy and those preparing couples for marriage might be able to hand them this book to help them think through the inseparable relationship between words and weddings, between poetry and possibility. At a time when many of us have lots to live with but little sense of what to live for, careful work needs to be done to help us speak words of commitment, words which reveal we have a will and potential. If the couple cannot find anything suitable here to enrich their celebration, I hope it will at least prompt a further search to discover readings which will help seal the truth of their love for one another. This reissue has a beautiful cover designed by Monica Capoferri, which recalls Edward Lear's Owl and Pussycat in their beautiful pea-green boat. Their wedding day ends perfectly, as does the poem:

> And hand in hand, on the edge of the sand
> They danced by the light of the moon,
> > The moon,
> > The moon,
> They danced by the light of the moon.

I hope that any poem or reading, carefully chosen by a couple, will prove to be a simple and vital part of their life through the years, and a continual reminder of the truth we know very deep down – that life enlarges in very unforeseen ways on the day when 'me' becomes 'us'.

Mark Oakley
St Paul's Cathedral

Bible Readings

Genesis 1.26–28, 31

In the image of God he created them

Then God said, 'Let us make humankind in our image, according to our likeness; and let them have dominion over the fish of the sea, and over the birds of the air, and over the cattle, and over all the wild animals of the earth, and over every creeping thing that creeps upon the earth.'

So God created humankind in his image, in the image of God he created them; male and female he created them.

God blessed them, and God said to them, 'Be fruitful and multiply, and fill the earth and subdue it; and have dominion over the fish of the sea and over the birds of the air and over every living thing that moves upon the earth.'. . .

God saw everything that he had made, and indeed, it was very good.

Genesis 2.18–24

They become one flesh

Then the Lord God said, 'It is not good that the man should be alone; I will make him a helper as his partner.' So out of the ground the Lord God formed every animal of the field and every bird of the air, and brought them to the man to see what he would call them; and whatever the man called every living creature, that was its name. The man gave names to all cattle, and to the birds of the air, and to every animal of the field; but for the man there was not found a helper as his partner. So the Lord God caused a deep sleep to fall upon the man, and he slept; then he took one of his ribs and closed up its place with flesh. And the rib that the Lord God had taken from the man he made into a woman and brought her to the man. Then the man said, 'This at last is one of my bones and flesh of my flesh; this one shall be called Woman, for out of Man this one was taken.' Therefore a man leaves his father and his mother and clings to his wife, and they become one flesh.

Genesis 24.48–51, 58–67

He took Rebekah, and she became his wife;
and he loved her.

The servant of Abraham said to Laban: 'Then I bowed
my head and worshipped the Lord, and blessed the
Lord, the God of my master Abraham, who had held me
by the right way to obtain the daughter of my master's
kinsman for his son. Now then, if you will deal loyally
and truly with my master, tell me; and if not, tell me, so
that I may turn to the right hand or to the left.'

Then Laban and Bethuel answered, 'The thing comes
from the Lord; we cannot speak to you anything bad or
good. Look, Rebekah is before you, take her and go, and
let her be the wife of your master's son, as the Lord has
spoken.'. . .

And they called Rebekah, and said to her, 'Will you
go with this man?' She said, 'I will.' So they sent away
their sister Rebekah and her nurse along with Abraham's
servant and his men. And they blessed Rebekah and
said to her, 'May you, our sister, become thousands of
myriads; may your offspring gain possession of the gates
of their foes.' Then Rebekah and her maids rose up,
mounted the camels, and followed the man; thus the
servant took Rebekah, and went his way.

Now Isaac had come from Beerlahai-roi, and was set-
tled in the Negeb. Isaac went out in the evening to walk
in the field; and looking up, he saw camels coming. And
Rebekah looked up, and when she saw Isaac, she slipped
quickly from the camel, and said to the servant, 'Who is
the man over there, walking in the field to meet us?' The

servant said, 'It is my master.' So she took her veil and covered herself. And the servant told Isaac all the things that he had done. Then Isaac brought her into his mother Sarah's tent. He took Rebekah, and she became his wife; and he loved her. So Isaac was comforted after his mother's death.

Ruth 1.16–18

Where you go, I will go

Ruth said, 'Do not press me to leave you or to turn back from following you! Where you go, I will go; where you lodge, I will lodge; your people shall be my people, and your God my God. Where you die, I will die – there will I be buried. May the Lord do thus and so to me, and more as well, if even death parts me from you!'

Psalm 67

God be merciful unto us, and bless us

God be merciful unto us, and bless us: and shew us the light of his countenance, and be merciful unto us;

That thy way may be known upon earth: thy saving health among all nations.

Let the people praise thee, O God: yea, let all the people praise thee.

O let the nations rejoice and be glad: for thou shalt judge the folk righteously, and govern the nations upon earth.

Let the people praise thee, O God: let all the people praise thee.

Then shall the earth bring forth her increase: and God, even our own God, shall give us his blessing.

God shall bless us: and all the ends of the world shall fear him.

(Book of Common Prayer)

Psalm *121*

I will lift up mine eyes unto the hills

I will lift up mine eyes unto the hills: from whence cometh my help.

My help cometh even from the Lord: who hath made heaven and earth.

He will not suffer thy foot to be moved: and he that keepeth thee will not sleep.

Behold, he that keepeth Israel: shall neither slumber nor sleep.

The Lord himself is thy keeper: the Lord is thy defence upon thy right hand;

So that the sun shall not burn thee by day: neither the moon by night.

The Lord shall preserve thee from all evil: yea, it is even he that shall keep thy soul.

The Lord shall preserve thy going out, and thy coming in: from this time forth for evermore.

(Book of Common Prayer)

Psalm 128

Blessed are all they that fear the Lord

Blessed are all they that fear the Lord: and walk in his ways.

For thou shalt eat the labours of thine hands: O well is thee, and happy shalt thou be.

Thy wife shall be as the fruitful vine: upon the walls of thine house.

Thy children like the olive-branches: round about thy table.

Lo, thus shall the man be blessed: that feareth the Lord.

The Lord from out of Sion shall so bless thee: that thou shalt see Jerusalem in prosperity all thy life long.

Yea, that thou shalt see thy children's children: and peace upon Israel.

(Book of Common Prayer)

Psalm 150

O praise God in his holiness

O praise God in his holiness: praise him in the firmament of his power.

Praise him in his noble acts: praise him according to his excellent greatness.

Praise him in the sound of the trumpet: praise him upon the lute and harp.

Praise him in the cymbals and dances: praise him upon the strings and pipe.

Praise him upon the well-tuned cymbals: praise him upon the loud cymbals.

Let every thing that hath breath: praise the Lord.

(Book of Common Prayer)

Song of Solomon 2.8–12; 8.6–7
Love is strong as death

The voice of my beloved!
   Look, he comes,
leaping upon the mountains,
   bounding over the hills.
My beloved is like a gazelle
   or a young stag.
Look, there he stands
   behind our wall,
gazing in at the windows,
   looking through the lattice.
My beloved speaks and says to me:
'Arise, my love, my fair one,
   and come away;
for now the winter is past,
   the rain is over and gone.
The flowers appear on the earth;
   the time of singing has come,
and the voice of the turtledove
   is heard in our land.'. . .

Set me as a seal upon your heart,
   as a seal upon your arm;
for love is strong as death,
   passion fierce as the grave.
Its flashes are flashes of fire,
   a raging flame.

Many waters cannot quench love,
   neither can floods drown it.
If one offered for love
   all the wealth of his house,
   it would be utterly scorned.

Jeremiah 31.31–34
I will be their God and they shall
be my people

The days are surely coming, says the Lord, when I will
make a new covenant with the house of Israel and the
house of Judah. It will not be like the covenant that I
made with their ancestors when I took them by the hand
to bring them out of the land of Egypt – a covenant that
they broke, though I was their husband, says the Lord.
But this is the covenant that I will make with the house
of Israel after those days, says the Lord: I will put my law
within them, and I will write it in their hearts; and I will
be their God, and they shall be my people. No longer
shall they teach one another, or say to each other, 'Know
the Lord', for they shall all know me, from the least of
them to the greatest, says the Lord.

Tobit 7.9–10, 11–14

Your marriage to her has been decided in heaven!

Tobiah said to Raphael, 'Brother Azariah, ask Raguel to let me marry my kinswoman Sarah.' Raguel overheard the words; so he said to the boy: 'Eat and drink and be merry tonight, for no man is more entitled to marry my daughter Sarah than you, brother. Besides, not even I have the right to give her to anyone but you, because you are my closest relative. But I will explain the situation to you very frankly . . . She is yours according to the decree of the Book of Moses. Your marriage to her has been decided in heaven! Take your kinswoman; from now on you are her love, and she is your beloved. She is yours today and ever after. And tonight, son, may the Lord of heaven prosper you both. May he grant you mercy and peace.' Then Raguel called his daughter Sarah, and she came to him. He took her by the hand and gave her to Tobiah with the words: 'Take her according to the law. According to the decree written in the Book of Moses she is your wife. Take her and bring her back safely to your father. And may the God of heaven grant both of you peace and prosperity.' He then called her mother and told her to bring a scroll, so that he might draw up a marriage contract stating that he gave Sarah to Tobiah as his wife according to the decree of the Mosaic law. Her mother brought the scroll, and he drew up the contract to which they affixed their seals.

Afterward they began to eat and drink.

(New American Bible)

Tobit 8.5–7

Allow us to live together to a happy old age

[On the wedding night Sarah] got up, and [she and Tobiah] started to pray and beg that deliverance might be theirs. He began with these words:

'Blessed are you, O God of our fathers;
praised be your name forever and ever.

Let the heavens and all your creation
praise you forever.

You made Adam and you gave him his wife Eve
to be his help and support;
and from these two the human race descended.

You said, "It is not good for the man to be alone;
let us make him a partner like himself."

Now, Lord, you know that I take this wife of mine
not because of lust,
but for a noble purpose.

Call down your mercy on me and on her,
and allow us to live together to a happy old age.'

(New American Bible)

Matthew 5.1–12

Blessed are the pure in heart

When Jesus saw the crowds, he went up the mountain; and after he sat down, his disciples came to him. Then he began to speak, and taught them, saying:

> Blessed are the poor in spirit, for theirs is the kingdom of heaven.
>
> Blessed are those who mourn, for they will be comforted.
>
> Blessed are the meek, for they will inherit the earth.
>
> Blessed are those who hunger and thirst for righteousness, for they will be filled.
>
> Blessed are the merciful, for they will receive mercy.
>
> Blessed are the pure in heart, for they will see God.
>
> Blessed are the peacemakers, for they will be called children of God.
>
> Blessed are those who are persecuted for righteousness' sake, for theirs is the kingdom of heaven.
>
> Blessed are you when people revile you and persecute you and utter all kinds of evil against you falsely on my account. Rejoice and be glad, for your reward is great in heaven, for in the same way they persecuted the prophets who were before you.

Matthew 5.13–16
Let your light shine

[Jesus said:] 'You are the salt of the earth; but if salt has lost its taste, how can its saltiness be restored? It is no longer good for anything, but is thrown out and trampled under foot.

'You are the light of the world. A city built on a hill cannot be hid. No one after lighting a lamp puts it under the bushel basket, but on the lampstand, and it gives light to all in the house. In the same way, let your light shine before others, so that they may see your good works and give glory to your Father in heaven.

Matthew 19.3–6

What God has joined together,
let no one separate

Some Pharisees came to him, and to test him they asked, 'Is it lawful for a man to divorce his wife for any cause?' He answered, 'Have you not read that the one who made them at the beginning made them male and female,' and said, "For this reason a man shall leave his father and mother and be joined to his wife, and the two shall become one flesh"? So they are no longer two, but one flesh. Therefore what God has joined together, let no one separate.'

Romans 8.35, 37–39
Who will separate us from the
love of Christ?

Who will separate us from the love of Christ? Will
hardship, or distress, or persecution, or famine, or
nakedness, or peril, or sword? . . . No, in all these things
we are more than conquerors through him who loved
us. For I am convinced that neither death, nor life, nor
angels, nor rulers, nor things present, nor things to
come, nor powers, nor height, nor depth, nor anything
in all creation will be able to separate us from the love
of God in Christ Jesus our Lord.

Romans 12.1–2, 9–18
Let love be genuine

I appeal to you, therefore, brothers and sisters, by the mercies of God, to present your bodies as a living sacrifice, holy and acceptable to God, which is your spiritual worship. Do not be conformed to this world, but be transformed by the renewing of your minds, so that you may discern what is the will of God – what is good and acceptable and perfect . . .

Let love be genuine; hate what is evil, hold fast to what is good; love one another with mutual affection; outdo one another in showing honour. Do not lag in zeal, be ardent in spirit, serve the Lord. Rejoice in hope, be patient in suffering, persevere in prayer. Contribute to the needs of the saints; extend hospitality to strangers.

Bless those who persecute you; bless and do not curse them. Rejoice with those who rejoice, weep with those who weep. Live in harmony with one another; do not be haughty, but associate with the lowly; do not claim to be wiser than you are. Do not repay anyone evil for evil, but take thought for what is noble in the sight of all. If it is possible, so far as it depends on you, live peaceably with all.

1 Corinthians 13.1–13
The greatest of these is love

If I speak in the tongues of mortals and of angels, but do not have love, I am a noisy gong or a clanging cymbal. And if I have prophetic powers, and understand all mysteries and all knowledge, and if I have all faith, so as to remove mountains, but do not have love, I am nothing. If I give away all my possessions, and if I hand over my body so that I may boast, but do not have love, I gain nothing.

Love is patient; love is kind; love is not envious or boastful or arrogant or rude. It does not insist on its own way; it is not irritable or resentful; it does not rejoice in wrongdoing, but rejoices in the truth. It bears all things, believes all things, hopes all things, endures all things.

Love never ends. But as for prophecies, they will come to an end; as for tongues, they will cease; as for knowledge, it will come to an end. For we know only in part, and we prophesy only in part; but when the complete comes, the partial will come to an end. When I was a child, I spoke like a child, I thought like a child, I reasoned like a child; when I became an adult, I put an end to childish ways. For now we see in a mirror, dimly, but then we will see face to face. Now I know only in part; then I will know fully, even as I have been fully known. And now faith, hope and love abide, these three; and the greatest of these is love.

Philippians 4.4–9

Let your gentleness be known to everyone

Rejoice in the Lord always; again I will say, rejoice. Let your gentleness be known to everyone. The Lord is near. Do not worry about anything, but in everything by prayer and supplication with thanksgiving let your requests be made known to God. And the peace of God, which surpasses all understanding, will guard your hearts and your minds in Christ Jesus.

Finally, beloved, whatever is true, whatever is honourable, whatever is just, whatever is pure, whatever is pleasing, whatever is commendable, if there is any excellence and if there is anything worthy of praise, think about these things. Keep on doing the things that you have learned and received and heard and seen in me, and the God of peace will be with you.

Colossians 3.12–15
Clothe yourselves with love

As God's chosen ones, holy and beloved, clothe yourselves with compassion, kindness, humility, meekness
and patience. Bear with one another and, if anyone has
a complaint against another, forgive each other; just as
the Lord has forgiven you, so you also must forgive.
Above all, clothe yourselves with love, which binds
everything together in perfect harmony. And let the
peace of Christ rule in your hearts, to which indeed you
were called in the one body. And be thankful.

1 *John* 3.18–24

Let us love in truth

Little children, let us love, not in word or speech, but in truth and action. And by this we will know that we are from the truth and will reassure our hearts before him whenever our hearts condemn us; for God is greater than our hearts, and he knows everything. Beloved, if our hearts do not condemn us, we have boldness before God; and we receive from him whatever we ask, because we obey his commandments and do what pleases him.

And this is his commandment, that we should believe in the name of his Son Jesus Christ and love one another, just as he has commanded us. All who obey his commandments abide in him, and he abides in them. And by this we know that he abides in us, by the Spirit that he has given us.

1 John 4.7–12
Love is from God

Beloved, let us love one another, because love is from God; everyone who loves is born of God and knows God. Whoever does not love does not know God, for God is love. God's love was revealed among us in this way: God sent his only Son into the world so that we might live through him. In this is love, not that we loved God but that he loved us and sent his Son to be the atoning sacrifice for our sins. Beloved, since God loved us so much, we also ought to love one another. No one has ever seen God; if we love one another, God lives in us, and his love is perfected in us.

Poems and Reflections

Now You Will Feel No Rain

Apache song

Now you will feel no rain,
for each of you will be a shelter to the other.

Now you will feel no cold,
for each of you will be warmth to the other.

Now there will be no loneliness,
for each of you will be a comfort to the other.

Now you are two persons,
but there is only one life before you.

Go now to your dwelling place,
to enter into the days of your togetherness.

And may your days be good
and long upon the earth.

Carry Her Over the Water

W. H. Auden

Carry her over the water,
  And set down under the tree,
Where the culvers white all day and all night,
  And the winds from every quarter,
Sing agreeably, agreeably, agreeably of love.

Put a gold ring on her finger,
  And press her close to your heart,
While the fish in the lake their snapshots take,
  And the frog, that sanguine singer,
Sings agreeably, agreeably, agreeably of love.

The streets shall all flock to your marriage,
  The houses turn around to look,
The tables and chairs say suitable prayers,
  And the horses drawing your carriage
Sing agreeably, agreeably, agreeably of love.

O Tell Me the Truth About Love
W. H. Auden

Some say that love's a little boy,
    And some say it's a bird,
Some say it makes the world go round,
    And some say that's absurd,
And when I asked the man next-door,
    Who looked as if he knew,
His wife got very cross indeed,
    And said it wouldn't do.

    Does it look like a pair of pyjamas,
      Or the ham in a temperance hotel?
    Does its odour remind one of llamas,
      Or has it a comforting smell?
    Is it prickly to touch as a hedge is,
      Or soft as eiderdown fluff?
    Is it sharp or quite smooth at the edges?
      O tell me the truth about love.

Our history books refer to it
    In cryptic little notes,
It's quite a common topic on
    The Transatlantic boats;
I've found the subject mentioned in
    Accounts of suicides,
And even seen it scribbled on
    The backs of railway-guides.

Does it howl like a hungry Alsatian,
    Or boom like a military band?
Could one give a first-rate imitation
    On a saw or a Steinway Grand?
Is its singing at parties a riot?
    Does it only like Classical stuff?
Will it stop when one wants to be quiet?
    O tell me the truth about love.

I looked inside the summer-house;
    It wasn't even there:
I tried the Thames at Maidenhead,
    And Brighton's bracing air.
I don't know what the blackbird sang,
    Or what the tulip said;
But it wasn't in the chicken-run,
    Or underneath the bed.

Can it pull extraordinary faces?
    Is it usually sick on a swing?
Does it spend all is time at the races?
    Or fiddling with pieces of string?
Has it views of its own about money?
    Does it think Patriotism enough?
Are its stories vulgar but funny?
    O tell me the truth about love.

When it comes, will it come without warning
    Just as I'm picking my nose?
Will it knock on my door in the morning,
    Or tread in the bus on my toes?

Will it come like a change in the weather?
    Will its greeting be courteous or rough?
Will it alter my life altogether?
    O tell me the truth about love.

From *Poetry and Marriage*
Wendell Berry

The meaning of marriage begins in the giving of words. We cannot join ourselves to another without giving our word. And this must be an unconditional giving, for in joining ourselves to one another we join ourselves to the unknown. We can join one another only by joining the unknown. We must not be misled by the procedures of experimental thought: in life, in the world, we are never given two known results to choose between, but only one result: that we choose without knowing what it is . . .

Because the condition of marriage is worldly and its meaning communal, no one party to it can be solely in charge. What you alone think it ought to be, it is not going to be. Where you alone think you want it to go, it is not going to go. It is going where the two of you – and marriage, time, life, history and the world – will take it. You do not know the road; you have committed your life to a way.

To My Dear and Loving Husband
Ann Bradstreet

If ever two were one, then surely we.
If ever man were lov'd by wife, then thee:
If ever wife was happy in a man,
Compare with me ye women if you can.
I prize thy love more than hole Mines of gold,
Or all the riches that the Earth dost hold.

My love is such that Rivers cannot quench,
Nor ought but love from thee, give recompense.
Thy love is such I can no way repay,
The heavens reward thee manifold I pray.
Then while we live, in love let's so persever,
That when we live no more, we may live ever.

Sonnet No. 19
Bertolt Brecht

My one requirement: that you stay with me.
I want to hear you, grumble as you may.
If you were deaf I'd need what you might say
If you were dumb I'd need what you might see.

If you were blind I'd want you in my sight
For you're the sentry posted to my side:
We're hardly half way through our lengthy ride
Remember we're surrounded yet by night.

Your 'let me lick my wounds' is no excuse now.
Your 'anywhere' (not here) is no defence
There'll be relief for you, but no release now.

You know whoever's needed can't go free
And you are needed urgently by me
I speak of me when us would make more sense.

(trans. John Willett)

How Do I love Thee?
Let Me Count the Ways
Elizabeth Barrett Browning

How do I love thee? Let me count the ways.
I love thee to the depth and breadth and height
My soul can reach, when feeling out of sight
For the ends of being and ideal grace.
I love thee to the level of every day's
Most quiet need, by sun and candlelight.
I love thee freely, as men strive for right;
I love thee purely, as they turn from praise.
I love thee with the passion put to use
In my old griefs, and with my childhood's faith.
I love thee with a love I seemed to lose
With my lost saints – I love thee with the breath,
Smiles, tears, of all my life! – and, if God choose,
I shall but love thee better after death.

Late Fragment
Raymond Carver

And did you get what
you wanted from this life, even so?
I did.
And what did you want?
To call myself beloved, to feel myself
beloved on the earth.

Che Fece ... Il Gran Rifiuto

C. P. Cavafy

For some people the day comes
when they have to declare the great Yes
or the great No. It's clear at once who has the Yes
ready within him; and saying it,

he goes from honour to honour, strong in his
    conviction.
He who refuses does not repent. Asked again,
he'd still say no. Yet that no – the right no –
drags him down all his life.

Patagonia
Kate Clanchy

I said *perhaps Patagonia*, and pictured
a peninsula, wide enough
for a couple of ladderback chairs
to wobble on at high tide. I thought

of us in breathless cold, facing
a horizon round as a coin, looped
in a cat's cradle strung by gulls
from sea to sun. I planned to wait

till the waves had bored themselves
to sleep, till the last clinging barnacles,
growing worried in the hush, had
paddled off in tiny coracles, till

those restless birds, your actor's hands,
had dropped slack into your lap,
until you'd turned, at last, to me.
When I spoke of Patagonia, I meant

skies all empty aching blue. I meant
years. I meant all of them with you.

After the Lunch

Wendy Cope

On Waterloo Bridge, where we said our goodbyes,
The weather conditions bring tears to my eyes.
I wipe them away with a black woolly glove
And try not to notice I've fallen in love.

On Waterloo Bridge, I am trying to think:
This is nothing. You're high on the charm and the drink.
But the juke-box inside me is playing a song
That says something different. And when was it
    wrong?

On Waterloo Bridge with the wind in my hair
I am tempted to skip. *You're a fool. I don't care.*
The head does its best but the heart is the boss –
I admit it before I am halfway across.

As Sweet
Wendy Cope

It's all because we're so alike –
Twin souls, we two.
We smile at the expression, yes,
And know it's true.

I told the shrink. He gave our love
A different name.
But he can call it what he likes –
It's still the same.

I long to see you, hear your voice,
My narcissistic object-choice.

Being Boring

Wendy Cope

'May you live in interesting times.'
Chinese curse

If you ask me 'What's new?', I have nothing to say
Except that the garden is growing.
I had a slight cold but it's better today.
I'm content with the way things are going.
Yes, he is the same as he usually is,
Still eating and sleeping and snoring.
I get on with my work. He gets on with his.
I know this is all very boring.

There was drama enough in my turbulent past:
Tears and passion – I've used up a tankful.
No news is good news, and long may it last,
If nothing much happens, I'm thankful.
A happier cabbage you never did see,
My vegetable spirits are soaring.
If you're after excitement, steer well clear of me.
I want to go on being boring.

I don't go to parties. Well, what are they for,
If you don't need to find a new lover?
You drink and you listen and drink a bit more
And you take the next day to recover.
Someone to stay home with was all my desire
And, now that I've found a safe mooring,
I've just one ambition in life: I aspire
To go on and on being boring.

Giving Up Smoking
Wendy Cope

There's not a Shakespeare sonnet
Or a Beethoven quartet
That's easier to like than you
Or harder to forget.

You think that sounds extravagant?
I haven't finished yet –
I like you more than I would like
To have a cigarette.

LVII

E. E. Cummings

somewhere i have never travelled,gladly beyond
any experience,your eyes have their silence:
in your most frail gesture are things which enclose me,
or which i cannot touch because they are too near

your slightest look easily will unclose me
though i have closed myself as fingers,
you open always petal by petal myself as Spring opens
(touching skilfully,mysteriously)her first rose

or if your wish be to close me,i and
my life will shut very beautifully,suddenly,
as when the heart of this flower imagines
the snow carefully everywhere descending;

nothing which we are to perceive in this world equals
the power of your intense fragility:whose texture
compels me with the colour of its countries,
rendering death and forever with each breathing

(i do not know what it is about you that closes
and opens;only something in me understands
the voice of your eyes is deeper than all roses)
nobody,not even the rain,has such small hands

The Anniversarie
John Donne

All Kings, and all their favourites,
    All glory of honours, beauties, wits,
The sun itself, which makes times, as they pass,
Is elder by a year now than it was
When thou and I first one another saw:
All other things to their destruction draw,
      Only our love hath no decay;
This no tomorrow hath, nor yesterday,
Running it never runs from us away,
But truly keeps his first, last, everlasting day.

    Two graves must hide thine and my coarse;
    If one might, death were no divorce.
Alas, as well as other Princes, we
(Who Prince enough in one another be)
Must leave at last in death these eyes and ears,
Oft fed with true oaths, and with sweet salt tears;
      But souls where nothing dwells but love
(All other thoughts being inmates) then shall prove
This, or a love increased there above,
Then bodies to their graves, souls from their graves
    remove.

    And then we shall be thoroughly blessed;
    But we no more than all the rest.
Here upon earth we're Kings, and none but we
Can be such Kings, nor of such subjects be;

Who is so safe as we? where none can do
Treason to us, except one of us two.
      True and false fears let us refrain,
Let us love nobly, and live, and add again
Years and years unto years, till we attain
To write threescore: this is our second of our reign.

The Good-morrow
John Donne

I wonder by my troth, what thou and I
Did, till we loved? were we not weaned till then?
But sucked on country pleasures, childishly?
Or snorted we in the seven sleepers' den?
'Twas so; but this, all pleasures fancies be.
If ever any beauty I did see,
Which I desired, and got, 'twas but a dream of thee.

And now good-morrow to our waking souls,
Which watch not one another out of fear;
For love all love of other sights controls,
And makes one little room an everywhere.
Let sea-discoverers to new worlds have gone,
Let maps to other, worlds on worlds have shown,
Let us possess one world, each hath one, and is one.

My face in thine eye, thine in mine appears,
And true plain hearts do in the faces rest;
Where can we find two better hemispheres
Without sharp North, without declining West?
What ever dies, was not mixed equally;
If our two loves be one, or thou and I
Love so alike that none do slacken, none can die.

A Dedication to My Wife
T. S. Eliot

To whom I owe the leaping delight
That quickens my senses in our wakingtime
And the rhythm that governs the repose of our
sleepingtime,
        The breathing in unison

Of lovers whose bodies smell of each other
Who think the same thoughts without need of speech
And babble the same speech without need of meaning.

No peevish winter wind shall chill
No sullen tropic sun shall wither
The roses in the rose-garden which is ours and ours
    only

But this dedication is for others to read:
These are private words addressed to you in public.

To Margo

Gavin Ewart

In life's rough-and-tumble
you're the crumble on my apple crumble
and the fairy on my Christmas tree!
In life's death-and-duty
you've the beauty of the Beast's own Beauty –
I feel humble as a bumble bee!

In life's darkening duel
I'm the lighter, you're the lighter fuel –
and the tide that sways my inland sea!
In life's meet-and-muster
you've the lustre of a diamond cluster –
a blockbuster – just a duster, me!

The Absent-Minded Lover's Apology
U. A. Fanthorpe

I would like you to think I love you warmly
Like brown cat yawning among sheets in the
    linen-cupboard.

I would like you to think I love you resourcefully
Like rooftop starlings posting chuckles down the flue.

I would like you to think I love you extravagantly
Like black cat embracing the floor when you pick up
    the tin-opener.

I would like you to think I love you accurately
Like Baskerville kern that fits its place to a T.

I would like you to think I love you with hurrahs and
    hallelujahs
Like dog gippetting at you down the intricate
    hillside.

I would like you to think I love you wittily
Like pottery Cox that lurks in the fruit-bowl under the
    Granny Smiths.

I would like you to think I love you pacifically and
    for ever
Like collared doves on the whitebeam's domestic
    branch.

I would like you to think I love you chronically
Like second hand solemnly circumnavigating the clock.

And O I want to love you, not in the absent tense, but
    in the here and the now
Like a present-minded lover.

Two Love Poems

Vicki Feaver

1.
listen:
it is said
and said again
continuously
like the sound of the sea
that is not sea
in the shell's ear

listen:
it is faint
so faint
that when the sea
turns like a mad thing
at the moon's whim
it is hard to hear

listen:
it is there
always there
always waiting
in the place
where it was left
for you to take again

listen:
it is said
and said again

until the day
you pick it up
and put it to your ear
and will not hear

2.
Sharing one umbrella
We have to hold each other
Round the waist to keep together.
You ask me why I'm smiling –
It's because I'm thinking
I want it to rain for ever.

Better Not

Erich Fried

Life
would perhaps
be easier
if I had
never met you

Less sadness
each time
when we must part
less fear
of the next parting
and the next after that

And not so much either
of this powerless longing
when you're not there

which wants only the
impossible
and that right away
next minute
and then
when that can't be
is hurt
and finds breathing difficult

Life
would perhaps be
simpler
If I hadn't met you
Only it wouldn't be
my life

From *The Prophet* (1)
Khalil Gibran

Love has no other desire but to fulfil itself.
But if you love and must needs have desires,
   let these be your desires:
To melt and be like a running brook that sings its
   melody to the night.
To know the pain of too much tenderness.
To be wounded by your own understanding of love;
And to bleed willingly and joyfully.
To wake at dawn with a winged heart and give thanks
   for another day of loving;
To rest at the noon hour and meditate love's ecstasy;
To return home at eventide with gratitude;
And then to sleep with a prayer for the beloved in
   your heart and a song of praise upon your lips.

From *The Prophet* (2)
Khalil Gibran

Then Almitra spoke again and said, And what of
    Marriage, master?
And he answered saying:
You were born together, and together you shall be for
    evermore.
You shall be together when the white wings of death
    scatter your days.
Aye, you shall be together even in the silent memory
    of God.
But let there be spaces in your togetherness,
And let the winds of the heavens dance between you.
Love one another but make not a bond of love:
Let it rather be a moving sea between the shores of
    your souls.
Fill each other's cup but drink not from one cup.
Give one another of your bread but eat not from the
    same loaf.
Sing and dance together and be joyous, but let each
    one of you be alone,
Even as the strings of a lute are alone though they
    quiver with the same music.
Give your hearts, but not into each other's keeping.
For only the hand of Life can contain your hearts.
And stand together yet not too near together:
For the pillars of the temple stand apart,
And the oak tree and cypress grow not in each other's
    shadow.

The Keyboard and the Mouse
Sophie Hannah

I am myself and in my house
But if I had my way
I'd be the keyboard and the mouse
Under your hands all day.

I'd be the C prompt on the screen.
We could have had some fun
This morning, if I'd only been
Word Perfect 5.1.

I'd be your hard and floppy disks,
I'd be your laser jet,
Your ampersands and asterisks –
I'd be in Somerset

Rotating on your swivel chair.
The journey takes a while
But press return and I'll be there.
Do not delete this file.

Friendship

Elizabeth Jennings

Such love I cannot analyse;
It does not rest in lips and eyes,
Neither in kisses nor caress.
Partly, I know, it's gentleness

And understanding in one word
Or in brief letters. It's preserved
By trust and by respect and awe.
These are the words I'm feeling for.

Two people, yes, two lasting friends.
The giving comes, the taking ends.
There is no measure for such things.
For this all Nature slows and sings.

Tell Me

Elizabeth Jennings

Tell me where you go
When you look faraway.
I find I am too slow

To catch your mood. I hear
The slow and far-off sea
And waves that beat a shore

That could be trying to
Call us toward our end,
make us hurry through

This little space of dark.
Yet love can stretch it wide.
Each life means so much work

You are my wealth, my pride.
The good side of me, see
That you stay by my side

Two roots of one great tree.

Husband to Wife: Party Going

Brian Jones

Turn where the stairs bend
In this other house; statued in other light,
Allow the host to ease you from your coat.
Stand where the stairs bend,
A formal distance from me, then descend
With delicacy conscious but not false
And take my arm, as if I were someone else.

Tonight, in a strange room
We will be strangers: let our eyes be blind
To all our customary stances –
Remark how well I'm groomed,
I will explore your subtly-voiced nuances
Where delicacy is conscious but not false,
And take your hand, as if you were someone else.

Home forgotten, rediscover
Among chirruping of voices, chink of glass,
Those simple needs that turned us into lovers,
How solitary was the wilderness
Until we met, took leave of hosts and guests,
And with delicate consciousness of what was false
Walked off together, as if there were no one else.

Benediction

Stanley Kunitz

God banish from your house
The fly, the roach, the mouse
That riots in the walls
Until the plaster falls;
Admonish from your door
The hypocrite and liar;
No shy, soft, tigrish fear
Permit upon your stair,
Nor agents of your doubt.
God drive them whistling out.
Let nothing touched with evil,
Let nothing that can shrivel
Heart's tendrest frond, intrude
Upon your still, deep blood.
Against the drip of night
God keep all windows tight,
Protect your mirrors from
Surprise, delirium,
Admit no trailing wind
Into your shuttered mind
To plume the lake of sleep
With dreams. If you must weep
God give you tears, but leave
You secrecy to grieve,
And islands for your pride,
And love to nest in your side.

A Lovely Song for Jackson
V. R. Lang

If I were a seaweed at the bottom of the sea,
I'd find you, and you'd find me.
Fishes would see us and shake their heads
Approvingly from their submarine beds.
Crabs and sea horses would bid us glad cry,
And sea anemone smile us by.
Sea gulls alone would wing and make moan,
Wondering, wondering, where we had gone.

If I were an angel and lost in the sun,
You would be there, and you would be one.
Birds that flew high enough would find us and sing
Gladder to find us than for anything,
And clouds would be proud of us, light everywhere
Would clothe us gold gaily, for dear and for fair.
Trees stretching skyward would see us and smile,
And all over heaven we'd laugh for a while.
Only the fishes would search and make moan,
Wondering, wondering, where we had gone.

The Owl and the Pussy Cat
Edward Lear

The Owl and the Pussy-Cat went to sea
    In a beautiful pea-green boat.
They took some honey, and plenty of money
    Wrapped up in a five pound note.
The Owl looked up to the stars above,
    And sang to a small guitar,
'O lovely Pussy! O Pussy, my love,
What a beautiful Pussy you are,
        You are,
        You are!
What a beautiful Pussy you are!'

Pussy said to the Owl, 'You elegant fowl!
    How charmingly sweet you sing!
O let us be married! too long we have tarried:
    But what shall we do for a ring?'
They sailed away, for a year and a day,
    To the land where the Bong-Tree grows,
And there in a wood a Piggy-wig stood,
With a ring at the end of his nose,
        His nose,
        His nose!
With a ring at the end of his nose.

'Dear Pig, are you willing to sell for one shilling
    Your ring?' Said the Piggy, 'I will.'
So they took it away, and were married next day
    By the turkey who lives on the hill.

They dined on mince, and slices of quince,
　　Which they ate with a runcible spoon;
And hand in hand, on the edge of the sand
They danced by the light of the moon,
　　　　The moon,
　　　　The moon,
They danced by the light of the moon.

Touching Your Face

Tom Leonard

with that
silence

it creates
allowing

and
trusting

the allowed;
all that's

been said
and is saying

this time
breath

held
between us

each time
familiar

each time
new

Sundaysong

Liz Lochhead

it's about time
it came back again
if it was going to.
yes   something's nesting
in the tentative creeper scribbling
Kellygreen felt tip
across our bedroom window.
hello.
it's a lovely morning.   we've got
full french roast for the enamelled yellow coffee pot.
there'll be transistors in the botanics
and blaring notes of blossom.
let's walk.   let's talk.
let the weekend watch wind down.
let there be sun
let first you and me
and then breakfast and lunch be
rolled into one.

To a Friend

Amy Lowell

I ask but one thing of you, only one,
That always you will be my dream of you;
That never shall I wake to find untrue
All this I have believed and rested on,
Forever vanished, like a vision gone
Out into the night. Alas, how few
There are who strike in us a chord we knew
Existed, but so seldom heard its tone
We tremble at the half-forgotten sound.
The world is full of rude awakenings
And heaven-born castles shattered to the ground,
yet still our human longing vainly clings
To a belief in beauty through all wrongs.
O stay your hand, and leave my heart its song!

From *Love in the Time of Cholera*
Gabriel Garcia Marquez

She clung to her husband. And it was just at the time when he needed her most, because he suffered the disadvantage of being ten years ahead of her as he stumbled alone through the mists of old age, with the even greater disadvantage of being a man and weaker than she was. In the end they knew each other so well that by the time they had been married for thirty years they were like a single divided being, and they felt uncomfortable at the frequency with which they guessed each other's thoughts without intending to, or the ridiculous accident of one of them anticipating in public what the other was going to say. Together they had overcome the daily incomprehension, the instantaneous hatred, the reciprocal nastiness and fabulous flashes of glory in the conjugal conspiracy. It was the time when they loved each other best, without hurry or excess, when both were most conscious of and grateful for their incredible victories over adversity. Life would still present them with other mortal trials, of course, but that no longer mattered: they were on the other shore.

Accidents of Birth

William Meredith

Spared by a car – or airplane – crash or
cured of malignancy, people look
around with new eyes at a newly
praiseworthy world, blinking eyes like these.

For I've been brought back again from the
fine silt, the mud where our atoms lie
down for long naps. And I've also been
pardoned miraculously for years
by the lava of chance which runs down
the world's gullies, silting us back.
Here I am, brought back, set up, not yet
happened away.

                         But it's not this random
life only, throwing its sensual
astonishments upside down on
the bloody membranes behind my eyeballs,
not just me being here again, old
needer, looking for someone to need,
but you, up from the clay yourself,
as luck would have it, and inching
over the same little eon, to
meet in a room, alive in our skins,
and the whole galaxy gaping there
and the centuries whining like gnats –
you, to teach me to see it, to see
it with you, and to offer somebody
uncomprehending, impudent thanks.

The Call

Charlotte Mew

From our low seat beside the fire
  Where we have dozed and dreamed and watched the
    glow
Or raked the ashes, stopping so
We scarcely saw the sun or rain
  Above, or looked much higher
Than this same quiet red or burned-out fire.
      To-night we heard a call,
      A rattle on the window-pane,
      A voice on the sharp air,
And felt a breath stirring our hair,
  A flame within us: Something swift and tall
  Swept in and out and that was all.
Was it a bright or dark angel? Who can know?
  It left no mark upon the snow,
      But suddenly it snapped the chain
      Unbarred, flung wide the door
      Which will not shut again;
And so we cannot sit here any more.
      We must arise and go:
      The world is cold without
      And dark and hedged about
      With mystery and enmity and doubt,
      But we must go
      Though yet we do not know
Who called, or what marks we shall leave upon the
  snow.

From *Now We Are Six*

A. A. Milne

Where ever I am, there's always Pooh,
There's always Pooh and Me.
Whatever I do, he wants to do,
'Where are you going today?' says Pooh:
'Well, that's very odd 'cos I was too.
Let's go together,' says Pooh, says he.
'Let's go together,' says Pooh.

'What's twice eleven?' I said to Pooh.
'Twice what?' said Pooh to Me.
'I think it ought to be twenty-two.'
'Just what I think myself,' said Pooh.
'It wasn't an easy sum to do,
But that's what it is,' said Pooh, said he.
'That's what it is,' said Pooh.

'Let's look for dragons,' I said to Pooh.
'Yes let's,' said Pooh to Me.
We crossed the river and found a few –
'Yes, those are dragons all right,' said Pooh.
'As soon as I saw their beaks I knew.
That's what they are,' said Pooh, said he.
'That's what they are,' said Pooh.

'Let's frighten the dragons,' I said to Pooh.
'That's right,' said Pooh to Me.
'I'm not afraid,' I said to Pooh.
And I held his paw and I shouted 'Shoo!

Silly old dragons!' – and off they flew.
'I wasn't afraid,' said Pooh, said he.
'I'm never afraid with you.'

Where ever I am, there's always Pooh,
There's always Pooh and Me.
'What would I do,' I said to Pooh.
'If it wasn't for you,' and Pooh said: 'True,
It isn't much fun for One, but Two
Can stick together,' says Pooh, says he.
'That's how it is,' says Pooh.

The Confirmation
Edwin Muir

Yes, yours, my love, is the right human face.
I in my mind had waited for this long,
Seeing the false and searching for the true,
Then found you as a traveller finds a place
Of welcome suddenly amid the wrong
Valleys and rocks and twisting roads. But you,
What shall I call you? A fountain in a waste,
A well of water in a country dry,
Or anything that's honest and good, an eye
That makes the whole world bright. Your open heart,
Simple with giving, gives the primal deed,
The first good world, the blossom, the blowing seed,
The hearth, the steadfast land, the wandering sea.
Not beautiful or rare in every part.
But like yourself, as they were meant to be.

From *The Book and the Brotherhood*
Iris Murdoch

I hereby give myself. I love you. You are the only being whom I can love absolutely with my complete self, with all my flesh and mind and heart. You are my mate, my perfect partner, and I am yours. You must feel this now, as I do . . . It was a marvel that we ever met. It is some kind of divine luck that we are together now. We must never, never part again. We are, here in this, necessary beings, like gods. As we look at each other we verify, we know, the perfection of our love, we recognize each other. Here is my life, here if need be is my death.

I Do, I Will, I Have

Ogden Nash

How wise I am to have instructed the butler to
    instruct
the first footman to instruct the second footman to
instruct the doorman to order my carriage;
I am about to volunteer a definition of marriage.
Just as I know that there are two Hagens, Walter and
    Copen,
I know that marriage is a legal and religious alliance
entered into by a man who can't sleep with the
    window
shut and a woman who can't sleep with the window
    open.
Moreover, just as I am unsure of the difference
    between
flora and fauna and flotsam and jetsam,
I am quite sure that marriage is the alliance of two
    people
one of whom never remembers birthdays and the other
    never forgetsam,
And he refuses to believe there is a leak in the water
    pipe
or the gas pipe and she is convinced she is about to
asphyxiate or drown,
And she says Quick get up and get my hairbrushes off
    the
windowsill, it's raining in, and he replies Oh they're all
right, it's only raining straight down.

That is why marriage is so much more interesting than
    divorce,
because it's the only known example of the happy
meeting of the immovable object and the irresistible
    force.
So I hope husbands and wives will continue to debate
    and
combat over everything debatable and combatable,
Because I believe a little incompatibility is the spice of
    life,
particularly if he has income and she is pattable.

To My Valentine
Ogden Nash

More than a catbird hates a cat,
Or a criminal hates a clue,
Or the Axis hates the United States,
That's how much I love you.

I love you more than a duck can swim,
And more than a grapefruit squirts,
I love you more than gin rummy is a bore,
And more than toothache hurts.

As a shipwrecked sailor hates the sea,
Or a juggler hates a shove,
As a hostess detests unexpected guests,
That's how much you I love.

I love you more than a wasp can sting,
And more than the subway jerks,
I love you as much as a beggar needs a crutch,
And more than a hangnail irks.

I swear to you by the stars above,
And below, if such there be,
As the High Court loathes perjurious oaths,
That's how you're loved by me.

We Don't Need To Leave Yet, Do We? Or, Yes We Do

Ogden Nash

One kind of person when catching a train always
   wants to allow an hour to cover the ten-block trip
   to the terminus.
And the other kind looks at them as if they were
   verminous.
And the second kind says that five minutes is plenty
   and will even leave one minute over for buying the
   tickets.
And the first kind looks at them as if they had cerebral
   rickets.
One kind when theatre-bound sups lightly at six and
   hastens off to the play,
And indeed I know one such person who is so such
   that it frequently arrives in time for the last act of
   the matinee,
And the other kind sits down at eight to a meal that is
   positively sumptuous,
Observing cynically that an eight-thirty curtain never
   rises till eight-forty, an observation which is less
   cynical than bumptuous.
And what the first kind, sitting uncomfortably in the
   waiting room while the train is made up in the
   yards, can never understand,
Is the injustice of the second kind's reaching their seat
   just as the train moves out, just as thy had planned,
And what the second kind cannot understand as they

stumble over the first kind's feet as the footlights
  flash on at last
Is that the first kind doesn't feel the least bit foolish at
  having entered the theatre before the cast.
Oh, the first kind always wants to start now and the
  second kind always wants to tarry,
Which wouldn't make any difference, except that each
  other is what they always marry.

From a Wedding Sermon
Mark Oakley

When I was training to be a priest I was sent to a church for a few weeks to work with an old, wise and gentle priest. He has since died. One Saturday, and I shall never forget this, he allowed me to stand next to him as he married a young couple who were obviously devoted to one another. After they had taken their vows and he had pronounced them husband and wife, the priest leaned forward and whispered so quietly to the man and woman that only they, and I, could hear. 'I have been married for fifty-one years,' he told them, 'but I don't have any secrets on how to keep a relationship like yours fresh. I want you to promise me, though, today, that you will always try and do three things. Always say to one another "I'm sorry"; and always say to each other "I forgive you"; and always, *please*, always keep telling one another "I love you".' I have never heard any better advice for such a beginning and I simply pass it on to you both today with hope and with much affection.

Quiet Song in Time of Chaos
Eugene O'Neill

Here
Is home.
Is peace.
Is quiet.

Here
Is love
That sits by the hearth
And smiles into the fire,
As into a memory
Of happiness,
As into the eyes
Of quiet.

Here
Is faith
That can be silent.
It is not afraid of silence.
It knows happiness
Is a deep pool
Of quiet.

Here
Sadness, too,
Is quiet.
Is the earth's sadness
On autumn afternoons
When days grow short,

And the year grows old,
When frost is in the air,
And suddenly one notices
Time's hair
Has grown whiter.

Here?
Where is here?
But you understand.
In my heart
Within your heart
Is home.
Is peace.
Is quiet.

It Takes Years to Marry

Theodore Parker

It takes years to marry completely two hearts, even of the most loving and well assorted. A happy wedlock is a long falling in love. Young persons think love belongs only to the brown-haired and crimson-cheeked. So it does for its beginning. But the golden marriage is a part of love which the Bridal day knows nothing of . . .

Such a large and sweet fruit is a complete marriage that it needs a long summer to ripen in, and then a long winter to mellow and season it. But a really happy marriage of love and judgment between a noble man and woman is one of the things so very handsome that if the sun were, as the Greeks once fabled, a God he might stop the world and hold it still now and then in order to look all day long on some example thereof, and feast his eyes on such a spectacle.

You're

Sylvia Plath

Clownlike, happiest on your hands,
Feet to the stars, and moon-skulled,
Gilled like a fish. A Common-sense
Thumbs-down on the dodo's mode.
Wrapped up in yourself like a spool,
Trawling your dark as owls do.
Mute as a turnip from the Fourth
Of July to All Fools' Day,
O high-riser, my little loaf.

Vague as fog and looked for like mail.
Farther off than Australia.
Bent-backed Atlas, our travelled prawn.
Snug as a bud and at home
Like a sprat in a pickle jug.
A creel of eels, all ripples.
Jumpy as a mexican bean.
Right, like a well-done sum.
A clean slate, with your own face on.

Sometimes

Sheenagh Pugh

Sometimes things don't go, after all,
from bad to worse. Some years, muscatel
faces down frost; green thrives; the crops don't fail.
Sometimes a man aims high, and all goes well.

A people sometimes will step back from war:
elect an honest man, decide they care
enough, that they can't leave some stranger poor.
Some men become what they were born for.

Sometimes our best efforts do not go
amiss; sometimes we do as we meant to.
The sun will sometimes melt a field of sorrow
that seemed hard frozen; may it happen for you.

From *Everything to Lose: Diaries 1945–1960*
Frances Partridge

May 4th 1948: I quite often look back at the pleasures and pains of youth – love, jealousy, recklessness, vanity – without forgetting their spell but no longer desiring them; while middle-aged ones like music, places, botany, conversation seem to be just as enjoyable as those wilder ones, in which there was usually some potential anguish lying in wait, like a bee in a flower. I hope there may be further surprises in store, and on the whole do not fear the advance into age . . .

May 5th: Ralph to London to the dentist. I have sprained my ankle so cannot go with him, but as the years pass I *hate* being parted from him even for an hour or so; I feel only half a person by myself, with one arm, one leg and half a face.

Warmer, softer, sweeter day: the birds sing very loudly and the pollarded trees on the road to Hungerford station seem to be holding little bunches of greenery in their fists.

A Birthday

Christina G. Rossetti

My heart is like a singing bird
    Whose nest is in a watered shoot;
My heart is like an apple tree
    Whose boughs are bent with thickset fruit;
My heart is like a rainbow shell
    That paddles in a halcyon sea;
My heart is gladder than all of these
    Because my love is come to me.

Raise me a dais of silk and down;
    Hang it with vair and purple dyes;
Carve it in doves and pomegranates
    And peacocks with a hundred eyes;
Work it in gold and silver grapes,
    In leaves and silver fleurs-de-lys;
Because the birthday of my life
    Is come, my love is come to me.

I Am Completely Different

Kuroda Saburo

I am completely different.
Though I am wearing the same tie as yesterday,
am as poor as yesterday,
as good for nothing as yesterday,
today
I am completely different.
Though I am wearing the same clothes,
am as drunk as yesterday,
living as clumsily as yesterday, nevertheless
today
I am completely different.

Ah –
I patiently close my eyes
on all the grins and smirks
on all the twisted smiles and horse laughs –
and glimpse then, inside me
one beautiful white butterfly
fluttering towards tomorrow.

Sonnet 29
William Shakespeare

When, in disgrace with fortune and men's eyes,
I all alone beweep my outcast state,
And trouble deaf heaven with my bootless cries,
And look upon myself, and curse my fate,
Wishing me like to one more rich in hope,
Featured like him, like him with friends possessed,
Desiring this man's art and that man's scope,
With what I most enjoy contented least;
Yet in these thoughts myself almost despising,
Haply I think on thee, and then my state,
Like to the lark at break of day arising
From sullen earth, sings hymns at heaven's gate;
    For thy sweet love remembered such wealth brings
    That then I scorn to change my state with kings.

Sonnet 116
William Shakespeare

Let me not to the marriage of true minds
Admit impediments. Love is not love
Which alters when it alteration finds,
Or bends with the remover to remove:
Oh no, it is an ever fixed mark
That looks on tempests and is never shaken;
It is the star to every wandering bark,
Whose worth's unknown, although his height be
    taken.
Love's not Time's fool, though rosy lips and cheeks
Within his bending sickle's compass come;
Love alters not with his brief hours and weeks,
But bears it out even to the edge of doom.
    If this be error and upon me proved,
    I never writ, nor no man ever loved.

Love's Philosophy
Percy Bysshe Shelley

The fountains mingle with the river
And the rivers with the ocean,
The winds of heaven mix for ever
With a sweet emotion;
Nothing in the world is single,
All things by a law divine
In one another's being mingle –
Why not I with thine?

See the mountains kiss high heaven
And the waves clasp one another;
No sister-flower would be forgiven
If it disdain'd its brother:

And the sunlight clasps the earth,
And the moonbeams kiss the sea –
What are all these kissings worth,
If thou kiss not me?

From A Marriage of True Minds
George Spater and Ian Parsons

[Virginia Woolf] said – and as though addressing herself rather than me [Bobo Mayer]: 'What do you think is probably the happiest moment in one's whole life?' While I was wondering how I should answer this sudden question, she went on, with a strange but very quiet radiance in her voice: 'I think it's the moment when one is walking in one's garden, perhaps picking off a few dead flowers, and suddenly one thinks: My husband lives in that house – And he loves me.' Her face shone as I had never seen it.

My Wife

Robert Louis Stevenson

Trusty, dusky, vivid, true,
With eyes of gold and bramble-dew,
Steel true and blade-straight,
The great artificer
Made my mate.

Honour, anger, valour, fire,
A love that life could never tire,
Death quench or evil stir;
The mighty master
Gave to her.

Teacher, tender, comrade, wife,
A fellow-farer true through life,
Heart-whole and soul-free,
The august father
Gave to me.

From *Virginibus Puerisque*
Robert Louis Stevenson

Love should run out to meet love with open arms. Indeed, the ideal story is that of two people who go into love step for step, with a fluttered consciousness, like a pair of children venturing together into a dark room. From the first moment when they see each other, with a pang of curiosity, through stage after stage of growing pleasure and embarrassment, they can read the expression of their own trouble in each other's eyes. There is no declaration properly so called; the feeling is so plainly shared, that as soon as the man knows what it is in his own heart, he is sure of what it is in the woman's.

Not Love Perhaps

A. S. J. Tessimond

This is not Love perhaps – Love that lays down
Its life, that many waters cannot quench, nor the
   floods drown –
But something written in lighter ink, said in a lower
   tone:
Something perhaps especially our own:
A need at times to be together and talk –
And then the finding we can walk
More firmly through dark narrow places
And meet more easily nightmare faces:
A need to reach out sometimes hand to hand –
And then find Earth less like an alien land:
A need for alliance to defeat
The whisperers at the corner of the street:
A need for inns on roads, islands in seas, halts for
   discoveries to be shared,
Maps checked and notes compared:
A need at times of each for each
Direct as the need of throat and tongue for speech.

After Years of Listening,
A Stone Comes to Life

James Tipton

After years of listening, a stone comes to life,
and the candle in the tiny grass;
and the night, like a wife, comes home;
a feather, in the touch of wind, flies back
to the lost bird, and everything I do not know
begins to sway at once.

I love these nights of irresistible somnambulance!
These nights when the wind blows its lullaby
to each lonely wing; I love this old body I walk in,
I love this dependable sage, this desert scent
I sink into when I rest; and suddenly I know
I will no longer apologise for loving you.

I whispered your name and the wind whinnied back.
All the horses of heaven are in the pasture tonight.

Gift

R. S. Thomas

Some ask the world
    and are diminished
in the receiving
    of it. You gave me

only this small pool
    that the more I drink
from, the more overflows
    me with sourceless light.

Dead Still

Andrei Voznesensky

Now, with your palms on the blades of my shoulders,
Let us embrace:
Let there be only your lips' breath on my face,
Only, behind our backs, the plunge of rollers.

Our backs, which like two shells in moonlight shine,
Are shut behind us now;
We lie here huddled, listening brow to brow,
Like life's twin formula or double sign.

In folly's world-wide wind
Our shoulders shield from the weather
The calm we now beget together,
Like a flame held between hand and hand.

Does each cell have a soul within it?
If so, fling open all your little doors,
And all your souls shall flutter like the linnet
In the cages of my pores.

Nothing is hidden that shall not be known.
Yet by no storm of scorn shall we
Be pried from this embrace, and left alone
Like muted shells forgetful of the sea.

Meanwhile, O load of stress and bother,
Lie on the shells of our backs in a great heap:
It will but press us closer, one to the other.

We are asleep.

(trans. Richard Wilbur)

The Mournes

Helen Waddell

I shall not go to heaven when I die.
But if they let me be
I think I'll take a road I used to know
That goes by Slieve-na-garagh and the sea.
And all day breasting me the wind will blow,
And I'll hear nothing but the peewit's cry
And the sea talking in the caves below.
I think it will be winter when I die
(For no-one from the North could die in Spring)
And all the heather will be dead and grey,
And the bog cotton will have blown away,
And there will be no yellow on the wind.
But I shall smell the peat
And when it's almost dark I'll set my feet
Where a white track goes glimmering to the hills,
And see, far up, a light
Would you think heaven could be so small a thing
As a lit window on the hills at night? –
And come in stumbling from the gloom,
Half blind, into a firelit room.
Turn, and see you
And there abide.

(If it were true
And if I thought that they would let me be
I almost wish it were tonight I died.)

The Old Words

David Wagoner

This is hard to say
Simply, because the words
Have grown so old together:
Lips and eyes and tears,
Touch and fingers
And love, out of love's language,
Are hard and smooth as stones
Laid bare in a streambed.
Not failing or fading
Like the halting speech of the body
Which will turn too suddenly
To ominous silence,
But like your lips and mine
Slow to separate, our fingers
Reluctant to come apart,
Our eyes and their slow tears
Reviving like these words
Springing to life again
And again, taken to heart.
To touch, love, to begin.

From *Tales of Men and Ghosts*
Edith Wharton

As her husband advanced up the path she had a sudden vision of their three years together. Those years were her whole life; everything before them had been colourless and unconscious, like the blind life of the plant before it reaches the surface of the soil. The years had not been exactly what she dreamed; but if they had taken away certain illusions they had left richer realities in their stead. She understood now that she had gradually adjusted herself to the new image of her husband as he was, as he would always be. He was not the hero of her dreams, but he was the man she loved, and who had loved her. For she saw now, in this last wide flash of pity and initiation, that, as a comely marble may be made out of worthless scraps of mortar, glass and pebbles, so out of mean mixed substances may be fashioned a love that will bear the stress of life.

He Wishes for the Cloths of Heaven
W. B. Yeats

Had I the heavens' embroidered cloths,
Enwrought with golden and silver light,
The blue and the dim and the dark cloths
Of night and light and the half-light,
I would spread the cloths under your feet:
But I, being poor, have only my dreams;
I have spread my dreams under your feet;
Tread softly because you tread on my dreams.

Hymns

All things bright and beautiful
C. F. Alexander

All things bright and beautiful,
  All creatures great and small,
All things wise and wonderful,
  The Lord God made them all.

Each little flower that opens,
  Each little bird that sings,
He made their glowing colours,
  He made their tiny wings.

The purple-headed mountain,
  The river running by,
The sunset and the morning,
  That brightens up the sky;

The cold wind in the winter,
  The pleasant summer sun,
The ripe fruits in the garden,
  He made them every one;

The tall trees in the greenwood,
  The meadows for our play,
The rushes by the water,
  To gather every day;

He gave us eyes to see them,
  And lips that we might tell
How great is God Almighty,
  Who has made all things well.

O *praise ye the Lord!*

H. W. Baker

O praise ye the Lord!
   Praise him in the height;
Rejoice in his word,
   Ye angels of light;
Ye heavens adore him
   By whom ye were made,
And worship before him,
   In brightness arrayed.

O praise ye the Lord!
   Praise him upon earth,
In tuneful accord,
   ye sons of new birth;
Praise him who has brought you
   His grace from above,
Praise him who has taught you
   To sing of his love.

O praise ye the Lord!
   All things that give sound;
Each jubilant chord,
   Re-echo around;
Loud organs, his glory
   Forth tell in deep tone,
And sweet harp, the story
   Of what he has done.

O praise ye the Lord!
   Thanksgiving and song
To him be outpoured
   All ages along:
For love in creation,
   For heaven restored,
For grace of salvation,
   O praise ye the Lord!

And did those feet in ancient time
William Blake

And did those feet in ancient time
   Walk upon England's mountains green?
And was the holy Lamb of God
   On England's pleasant pastures seen?
And did the countenance divine
   Shine forth upon our clouded hills?
And was Jerusalem builded here
   Among those dark satanic mills?

Bring me my bow of burning gold!
   Bring me my arrows of desire!
Bring me my spear! O clouds, unfold!
   Bring me my chariot of fire!
I will not cease from mental fight,
   Nor shall my sword sleep in my hand,
Till we have built Jerusalem
   In England's green and pleasant land.

O Jesus, I have promised

John Bode

O Jesus, I have promised
  To serve thee to the end;
Be thou for ever near me,
  My Master and my Friend;
I shall not fear the battle
  If thou art by my side,
Nor wander from the pathway
  If thou wilt be my guide.

O let me hear thee speaking
  In accents clear and still,
Above the storms of passion,
  The murmurs of self-will;
O speak to reassure me,
  To hasten or control;
O speak, and make me listen,
  Thou guardian of my soul.

O Jesus, thou hast promised
  To all who follow thee,
That where thou art in glory
  There shall thy servant be;
And, Jesus, I have promised
To serve thee to the end;
O give me grace to follow,
  My Master and my Friend.

O let me see thy footmarks,
    And in them plant my own;
My hope to follow duly
    Is in thy strength alone;
O guide me, call me, draw me,
    Uphold me to the end;
And then in heaven receive me,
    My Saviour and my Friend.

He who would valiant be
John Bunyan

He who would valiant be
'Gainst all disaster,
Let him in constancy
    Follow the Master.
There's no discouragement
Shall make him once relent
His first avowed intent
    To be a pilgrim.

Who so beset him round
With dismal stories,
Do but themselves confound
    His strength the more is.
No foes shall stay his might,
Though he with giants fight:
He will make good his right
    To be a pilgrim.

Since, Lord, thou dost defend
Us with thy Spirit,
We know we at the end
    Shall life inherit.
Then fancies flee away!
I'll fear not what men say,
I'll labour night and day
    To be a pilgrim.

I danced in the morning
Sydney Carter

I danced in the morning when the world was begun,
And I danced in the moon and the stars and the sun,
I came down from heaven and I danced on the earth;
At Bethlehem I had my birth.

Dance, then, wherever you may be;
I am the Lord of the Dance, said he,
And I'll lead you all, wherever you may be,
And I'll lead you all in the dance, said he.

I danced for the scribe and the pharisee,
But they would not dance and they would not follow me.
I danced for the fishermen, for James and John –
They came with me and the dance went on.

I danced on the Sabbath and I cured the lame;
The holy people said it was a shame.
They whipped and they stripped and they hung me on
   high;
They left me there on a cross to die.

I danced on a Friday when the sky turned black –
It's hard to dance with the devil on your back.
They buried my body and they thought I'd gone;
But I am the dance and I still go on.

They cut me down and I leapt up high;
I am the life that will never, never die;
I'll live in you if you'll live in me –
I am the Lord of the Dance said he.

Immortal, invisible, God only wise

W. Chalmers Smith

Immortal, invisible, God only wise,
In light inaccessible hid from our eyes,
Most blessed, most glorious, the Ancient of Days,
Almighty, victorious, thy great name we praise.

Unresting, unhasting, and silent as light,
Nor wanting, nor wasting, thou rulest in might;
Thy justice like mountains high soaring above
Thy clouds which are fountains of goodness and love.

To all life thou givest – to both great and small;
In all life thou livest, the true life of all;
We blossom and flourish as leaves on the tree,
And wither and perish – but nought changeth thee.

Great Father of glory, pure Father of light,
Thine angels adore thee, all veiling their sight;
All laud we would render: O help us to see
'Tis only the splendour of light hideth thee.

Come down, O Love divine

Bianco da Siena

Come down, O Love divine,
Seek thou this soul of mine,
And visit it with thine own ardour glowing;
O Comforter, draw near,
Within my heart appear,
And kindle it, thy holy flame bestowing.

O let it freely burn,
Till earthly passions turn
To dust and ashes in its heat consuming;
And let thy glorious light
Shine ever on my sight,
And clothe me round, the while my path illuming.

Let holy charity
Mine outward vesture be,
And lowliness become mine inner clothing;
True lowliness of heart,
Which takes the humbler part,
And o'er its own shortcomings weeps with loathing.

And so the yearning strong,
With which the soul will long,
Shall far outpass the power of human telling;
For none can guess its grace,
Till he become the place
Wherein the Holy Spirit makes his dwelling.

(trans. R. F. Littledale)

Tell out, my soul
Timothy Dudley-Smith

Tell out, my soul, the greatness of the Lord:
  Unnumbered blessings, give my spirit voice;
Tender to me the promise of his word;
  In God my Saviour shall my heart rejoice.

Tell out, my soul, the greatness of his name:
  Make known his might, the deeds his arm has done;
His mercy sure, from age to age the same;
  His holy name, the Lord, the Mighty One.

Tell out, my soul, the greatness of his might:
  Powers and dominions lay their glory by;
Proud hearts and stubborn wills are put to flight,
  The hungry fed, the humble lifted high.

Tell out, my soul, the glories of his word:
  Firm is his promise, and his mercy sure.
Tell out, my soul, the greatness of the Lord
  To children's children and for evermore.

Lead us, heavenly Father, lead us

James Edmeston

Lead us, heavenly Father, lead us
  O'er the world's tempestuous sea;
Guard us, guide us, keep us, feed us,
  For we have no help but thee;
Yet possessing every blessing
  If our God our Father be.

Saviour, breathe forgiveness o'er us,
  All our weakness thou dost know;
Thou didst tread this earth before us,
  Thou didst feel its keenest woe;
Self denying, death defying,
  Thou to Calvary didst go.

Spirit of our God, descending,
  Fill our hearts with heavenly joy;
Love with every passion blending,
  Pleasure that can never cloy;
Thus provided, pardoned, guided,
  Nothing can our peace destroy.

Morning has broken
Eleanor Farjeon

Morning has broken
Like the first morning,
Blackbird has spoken
  Like the first bird.
      Praise for the singing,
      Praise for the morning,
      Praise for them springing
        Fresh from the Word.

Sweet the rain's new fall
Sunlit from heaven,
Like the first dewfall
  On the first grass.
      Praise for the sweetness
      Of the wet garden,
      Sprung in completeness
        Where his feet pass.

Mine is the sunlight,
Mine is the morning
Born of the one light
  Eden saw play.
      Praise with elation,
      Praise every morning,
      God's re-creation
        Of the new day.

Make me a channel of your peace
St Francis of Assisi

Make me a channel of your peace.
Where there is hatred let me bring your love;
Where there is injury, your pardon, Lord;
And where there's doubt, true faith in You.

O Master, grant that I may never seek
So much to be consoled as to console;
To be understood as to understand;
To be loved, as to love with all my soul.

Make me a channel of your peace.
Where there's despair in life let me bring hope;
Where there is darkness, only light;
And where's sadness ever joy.

O Master . . .

Make me a channel of your peace.
It is in pardoning that we are pardoned,
In giving to all men that we receive;
And in dying that we're born to eternal life.

O Master . . .

(arr. Sebastian Temple)

O worship the King

Robert Grant

O worship the King
  All glorious above;
O gratefully sing
  His power and his love:
Our Shield and Defender,
  The Ancient of days,
Pavilion'd in splendour,
  And girded with praise.

O tell of his might,
  O sing of his grace,
Whose robe is the light,
  Whose canopy space.
His chariots of wrath
  The deep thunder-clouds form,
And dark is his path
  On the wings of the storm.

This earth, with its store
  Of wonders untold,
Almighty, thy power
  Hath founded of old:
Hath stablished it fast
  By a changeless decree,
And round it hath cast,
  Like a mantle, the sea.

Thy bountiful care
   What tongue can recite?
It breathes in the air,
   It shines in the light;
It streams from the hills,
   It descends to the plain,
And sweetly distils
   In the dew and the rain.

Frail children of dust,
   And feeble as frail,
In thee do we trust,
   Nor find thee to fail;
Thy mercies how tender!
   How firm to the end!
Our maker, Defender,
   Redeemer and Friend.

O measureless Might,
   Ineffable Love,
While angels delight
   To hymn thee above,
Thy humbler creation,
   Though feeble their lays,
With true adoration
   Shall sing to thy praise.

O perfect Love, all human thought transcending

Dorothy F. Gurney

O perfect Love, all human thought transcending,
   Lowly we kneel in prayer before thy throne,
That theirs may be the love that knows no ending
   Whom thou for evermore dost join in one.

O perfect Life, be thou their full assurance
   Of tender charity and steadfast faith,
Of patient hope, and quiet brave endurance,
   With childlike trust that fears nor pain nor death.

Grant them the joy that brightens earthly sorrow,
   Grant them the peace which calms all earthly strife;
And to life's day the glorious unknown morrow
   That dawns upon eternal love and life.

King of glory, King of peace

George Herbert

King of glory, King of peace,
    I will love thee;
And that love may never cease,
    I will move thee.
Thou hast granted my request,
    Thou hast heard me;
Thou didst note my working breast,
    Thou hast spared me.

Wherefore with my utmost art
    I will sing thee,
And the cream of all my heart
    I will bring thee.
Though my sins against me cried,
    Thou didst clear me;
And alone, when they replied,
    Thou didst hear me.

Seven whole days, not one in seven,
    I will praise thee;
In my heart, though not in heaven,
    I can raise thee.
Small it is, in this poor sort
    To enrol thee:
E'en eternity's too short
    To extol thee.

Let all the world in every corner sing
George Herbert

Let all the world in every corner sing,
    My God and King!
  The heavens are not too high,
  His praise may thither fly;
  The earth is not too low,
  His praises there may grow.
Let all the world in every corner sing,
    My God and King!

Let all the world in every corner sing,
    My God and King!
  The Church with psalms must shout,
  No door can keep them out;
  But above all, the heart
  Must bear the longest part.
Let all the world in every corner sing,
    My God and King!

Be thou my vision, O Lord of my heart
Eleanor Hull

Be thou my vision, O Lord of my heart,
Be all else but naught to me, save that thou art,
Be thou my best thought in the day and the night,
Both waking and sleeping, thy presence my light.

Be thou my wisdom, be thou my true word
be thou ever with me, and I with thee, Lord,
Be thou my great father, and I thy true son,
Be thou in me dwelling, and I with thee one.

Be thou my breastplate, my sword for the fight,
Be thou my whole armour, be thou my true might,
Be thou my soul's shelter, be thou my strong tower,
O raise thou me heavenward, great Power of my power.

Riches I heed not, nor man's empty praise,
Be thou my inheritance now and always,
Be thou and thou only the first in my heart,
O Sovereign of heaven, my treasure thou art.

High King of heaven, thou heaven's bright Sun,
O grant me its joys after vict'ry is won,
Great Heart of my own heart, whatever befall,
Still be thou my vision, O Ruler of all.

Praise, my soul, the King of heaven
H. F. Lyte

Praise, my soul, the King of heaven;
    To his feet thy tribute bring.
Ransomed, healed, restored, forgiven,
    Who like me his praise should sing?
        Praise him! Praise him!
    Praise the everlasting King.

Praise him for his grace and favour
    To our fathers in distress;
Praise him still the same for ever,
    Slow to chide and swift to bless.
        Praise him! Praise him!
    Glorious in his faithfulness.

Father-like, he tends and spares us;
    Well our feeble frame he knows;
In his hands he gently bears us,
    Rescues us from all our foes.
        Praise him! Praise him!
    Widely as his mercy flows.

Angels, help us to adore him;
    Ye behold him face to face;
Sun and moon, bow down before him;
    Dwellers all in time and space.
        Praise him! Praise him!
    Praise with us the God of grace.

O Love that wilt not let me go

George Matheson

O Love that wilt not let me go,
I rest my weary soul in Thee;
I give Thee back the life I owe,
that in Thine ocean depths its flow
may richer, fuller be.

O Light that followest all my way,
I yield my flickering torch to Thee;
my heart restores its borrowed ray,
that in Thy sunshine's blaze its day
may brighter, fairer be.

O Joy that seekest me through pain,
I cannot close my heart to Thee;
I trace the rainbow through the rain,
and feel the promise is not vain
that morn shall tearless be.

O Cross that liftest up my head,
I dare not ask to fly from Thee;
I lay in dust life's glory dead,
and from the ground there blossoms red
life that shall endless be.

Angel-voices ever singing

Francis Pott

Angel-voices ever singing
   Round thy throne of light,
Angel-harps for ever ringing,
   rest not day nor night;
Thousands only live to praise thee
   And confess thee
      Lord of might.

Thou who art beyond the farthest
   Mortal eye can scan,
Can it be that you regardest
   Songs of sinful man?
Can we know that you art near us,
   And wilt hear us?
      Yes, we can.

For we know that thou rejoicest
   O'er each work of thine;
Thou didst ears and hands and voices
   For thy praise design;
Craftsman's art and music's measure
   For thy pleasure
      All combine.

In thy house, great God, we offer
   Of thine own to thee;
And for thine acceptance proffer
   All unworthily

Hearts and minds and hands and voices
  In our choicest
      Psalmody.

Honour, glory, might and merit
  Thine shall ever be,
Father, Son and Holy Spirit,
  Blessed Trinity.
Of the best which thou hast given
  Earth and heaven
      Render thee.

God is Love: let heav'n adore him
Timothy Rees

God is Love: let heav'n adore him;
   God is Love: let earth rejoice;
Let creation sing before him,
   And exalt him with one voice.
He who laid the earth's foundation,
   He who spread the heav'ns above,
He who breathes through all creation,
   He is Love, eternal Love.

God is Love: and he enfoldeth
   All the world in one embrace;
With unfailing grasp he holdeth
   Every child of every race.
And when human hearts are breaking
   Under sorrow's iron rod,
Then they find that selfsame aching
   Deep within the heart of God.

God is Love: and though with blindness
   Sin afflicts the souls of men,
God's eternal loving-kindness
   Holds and guides them even then.
Sin and death and hell shall never
   O'er us final triumph gain;
God is Love, so Love for ever
   O'er the universe must reign.

Now thank we all our God
Martin Rinkart

Now thank we all our God,
With heart and hands and voices,
   Who wondrous things hath done,
In whom his world rejoices;
   Who from our mother's arms
      Hath blessed us on our way
   With countless gifts of love,
      And still is ours to-day.

O may this bounteous God
Through all our life be near us,
   With ever joyful hearts
And blessed peace to cheer us;
   And keep us in his grace,
      And guide us when perplexed,
   And free us from all ills
      In this world and the next.

All praise and thanks to God
The Father now be given,
   The Son, and him who reigns
With them in highest heaven,
   The One eternal God,
      Whom earth and heaven adore;
   For thus it was, is now,
      And shall be evermore.

(trans. Catherine Winkworth)

The Lord's my shepherd

Scottish Psalter

The Lord's my shepherd, I'll not want;
    He makes me down to lie
In pastures green; he leadeth me
    The quiet waters by.

My soul he doth restore again,
    And me to walk doth make
Within the paths of righteousness,
    E'en for his own name's sake.

Yea, though I walk in death's dark vale,
    yet will I fear no ill:
For thou art with me, and thy rod
    And staff me comfort still.

My table thou hast furnished
    In presence of my foes;
My head thou dost with oil anoint
    And my cup overflows.

Goodness and mercy all my life
    Shall surely follow me;
And in God's house for evermore
    My dwelling-place shall be.

Lord of all hopefulness

Jan Struther

Lord of all hopefulness, Lord of all joy,
Whose trust, ever child-like, no cares could destroy,
Be there at our waking, and give us, we pray,
Your bliss in our hearts, Lord, at the break of the day.

Lord of all eagerness, Lord of all faith,
Whose strong hands were skilled at the plane and the
    lathe,
Be there at our labours, and give us, we pray,
Your strength in our hearts, Lord, at the noon of the
    day.

Lord of all kindliness, Lord of all grace,
Your hands swift to welcome, your arms to embrace,
Be there at our homing, and give us, we pray,
Your love in our hearts, Lord, at the eve of the day.

Lord of all gentleness, Lord of all calm,
Whose voice is contentment, whose presence is balm,
Be there at our sleeping, and give us, we pray,
Your peace in our hearts, Lord, at the end of the day.

Love Divine, all loves excelling
Charles Wesley

Love Divine, all loves excelling,
  Joy of heaven, to earth come down,
Fix in us thy humble dwelling,
  All thy faithful mercies crown.
Jesu, thou art all compassion,
  Pure unbounded love thou art;
Visit us with thy salvation,
  Enter every trembling heart.

Come, almighty to deliver,
  Let us all thy life receive;
Suddenly return, and never,
  Never more thy temples leave.
Thee we would be always blessing,
  Serve thee as thy hosts above,
Pray, and praise thee, without ceasing,
  Glory in thy perfect love.

Finish then thy new creation,
  Pure and spotless let us be;
Let us see thy great salvation,
  Perfectly restored in thee,
Changed from glory into glory,
  Till in heaven we take our place,
Till we cast our crowns before thee,
  Lost in wonder, love, and praise!

O thou who camest from above
Charles Wesley

O thou who camest from above,
   The pure celestial fire to impart,
Kindle a flame of sacred love
   On the mean altar of my heart.

There let it for thy glory burn
   With inextinguishable blaze,
And trembling to its source return
   In humble prayer, and fervent praise.

Jesus, confirm my heart's desire
   To work, and speak, and think for thee;
Still let me guard the holy fire,
   And still stir up thy gift in me.

Ready for all thy perfect will,
   My acts of faith and love repeat,
Till death thy endless mercies seal,
   And make my sacrifice complete.

Guide me, O thou great Redeemer
William Williams

Guide me, O thou great Redeemer,
  Pilgrim through this barren land;
I am weak, but thou art mighty,
  Hold me with thy powerful hand:
    Bread of heaven,
Feed me till I want no more.

Open now the crystal fountain
  Whence the healing stream doth flow;
Let the fire and cloudy pillar
  Lead me all my journey through:
    Strong deliverer,
Be thou still my strength and shield.

When I tread the verge of Jordan,
  Bid my anxious fears subside;
Death of death, and hell's Destruction
  Land me safe on Canaan's side:
    Songs of praises
I will ever give to thee.

(trans. Peter Williams)

Dear Lord and Father of mankind
John Whittier

Dear Lord and Father of mankind,
  Forgive our foolish ways!
Re-clothe us in our rightful mind,
In purer lives thy service find,
  In deeper reverence praise.

In simple trust like theirs who heard,
  Beside the Syrian sea,
The gracious calling of the Lord,
Let us, like them, without a word
  Rise up and follow thee.

O Sabbath rest by Galilee!
  O calm of hills above,
Where Jesus knelt to share with thee
The silence of eternity,
  Interpreted by love!

Drop thy still dews of quietness,
  Till all our strivings cease;
Take from our souls the strain and stress,
And let our ordered lives confess
  The beauty of thy peace.

Breathe through the heats of our desire
  Thy coolness and thy balm;
Let sense be dumb, let flesh retire;
Speak through the earthquake, wind, and fire,
  O still small voice of calm!

Acknowledgements

The compiler and publisher are grateful for permission to include the following copyright material in this volume. Every effort has been made to trace the owners of copyright material, but if any errors or omissions still remain, we would ask those concerned to contact the publisher, who will ensure that full acknowledgement is made in future editions.

Unless otherwise stated, Scripture quotations are from the New Revised Standard Version of the Bible, copyright © 1989 by the Division of Christian Education of the National Council of the Churches of Christ in the USA. Used by permission. All rights reserved.

Extracts from The Book of Common Prayer, the rights in which are vested in the Crown, are reproduced by permission of the Crown's Patentee, Cambridge University Press.

Excerpts from the *New American Bible with Revised New Testament and Revised Psalms* are copyright © 1991, 1986, 1970 Confraternity of Christian Doctrine, Washington, D.C. and are used by permission of the copyright owner. All rights reserved.

W. H. Auden, 'Carry Her Over the Water', from *Ten Songs*, published by Faber & Faber Ltd.

W. H. Auden, 'O Tell Me the Truth About Love', from *Collected Shorter Poems*, published by Faber & Faber Ltd.

Bertolt Brecht, 'Sonnet 19', from *Poems 1913–1956*, translated by John Willett and Ralph Manheim, published by Methuen Publishing Ltd. Copyright © Bertolt-Brecht-Erben / Suhrkamp Verlag.

Sydney Carter, 'I danced in the morning', Sydney Carter © 1963, Stainer & Bell Ltd, London, England.

Raymond Carver, 'Late Fragment', from *All of Us: The Collected Poems*, published by The Harvill Press and © Tess Gallagher. Used by permission of The Random House Group Limited.

C. P. Cavafy, 'Che Fece . . . Il Gran Rifiuto' from *Collected Poems*, translated by Edmund Keeley and Philip Sherrard and published by Hogarth Press (1975). Used by permission of the Estate of C. P. Cavafy and The Random House Group Ltd.

Kate Clanchy, 'Patagonia', from *Hand in Hand*, edited by Carol Ann Duffy, published by Macmillan London.

Wendy Cope, 'After the Lunch', from *Serious Concerns*, published by Faber & Faber Ltd, 1992.

Wendy Cope, 'As Sweet', from *Serious Concerns*, published by Faber & Faber Ltd, 1992.

Wendy Cope, 'Being Boring', from *If I Don't Know*, published by Faber & Faber Ltd, 2001.

Wendy Cope, 'Giving Up Smoking', from *If I Don't Know*, published by Faber & Faber Ltd, 2001.

E. E. Cummings, 'somewhere i have never travelled, gladly beyond' is reprinted from *Complete Poems 1934–1963*, by E. E. Cummings, edited by George J. Firmage, by permission of

W. W. Norton and Company. Copyright © 1991 by the Trustees for the E. E. Cummings Trust and George James Firmage.

Timothy Dudley-Smith, 'Tell out my soul'. Text © Timothy Dudley-Smith in Europe (including UK and Ireland) and in all territories not controlled by Hope Publishing Company.

T. S. Eliot, 'A Dedication to My Wife', from *The Complete Poems and Plays*, published by Faber & Faber Ltd.

Gavin Ewart, 'To Margo', reprinted by kind permission of Mrs Margo Ewart.

U. A. Fanthorpe, 'The Absent-Minded Lover's Apology', copyright U. A. Fanthorpe, *Safe as Houses* (1995). Reproduced by permission of Peterloo Poets.

Eleanor Farjeon, 'Morning has broken', from *The Children's Bells* © Eleanor Farjeon and Oxford University Press.

Vicki Feaver, 'Two Love Poems' © Vicki Feaver, in *Close Relatives*, published by Secker, 1981.

Erich Fried, 'Better Not', from *Love Poems*, published by Calder Publications Ltd, 1991.

Sophie Hannah, 'The Keyboard and the Mouse', from *The Hero and the Girl Next Door*, published by Carcanet Press Ltd, 1995.

Eleanor Hull, 'Be thou my vision', from *The Poem of the Gael*, translated by M. E. Byrne and edited by Eleanor Hull. Originally published by Chatto & Windus. Reprinted by permission of The Random House Group Limited. Copyright © Eleanor Hull.

Elizabeth Jennings, 'Friendship' and 'Tell Me', from *Collected Poems*, published by Carcanet Press Ltd, 1987.

Brian Jones, 'Husband to Wife: Party Going', from *Poems*, published by Carcanet Press Ltd.

V. R. Lang, 'A Lovely Song for Jackson', from *Poems and Plays*, published by Heinemann. Used by permission of The Random House Group Ltd.

Tom Leonard, 'Touching Your Face', from *Hand in Hand*, edited by Carol Ann Duffy, published by Macmillan London.

Liz Lochhead, 'Sundaysong', from *Dreaming Frankenstein and Collected Poems*, published by Polygon Press, 1998. Permission sought from Liz Lochhead.

William Meredith, 'Accidents of Birth' is reprinted from *Effort at Speech: New and Selected Poems* by William Meredith, published by TriQuarterly Books/Northwestern University Press in 1997. Copyright © 1997 by William Meredith. All rights reserved. Used by permission of Northwestern University Press and Richard Harteis.

A. A. Milne, extract from *Now We Are Six* © A. A. Milne. Copyright under the Berne Convention. Published by Egmont Books Limited, London and used with permission.

Edwin Muir, 'The Confirmation', from *Collected Poems*, published by Faber & Faber Ltd.

Ogden Nash, 'To My Valentine', 'We Don't Need to Leave Yet, Do We?' and 'I Do, I Will, I Have', from *Candy is Dandy*, published by André Deutsch.

Eugene O'Neill, 'Quiet Song in Time of Chaos', from *Poems 1912–44* by Eugene O'Neill, published by Jonathan Cape. Reprinted by permission of The Random House Group Ltd.

Sylvia Plath, 'You're', from *Ariel*, published by Faber & Faber Ltd, 1965.

Sheenagh Pugh, 'Sometimes', from *Selected Poems*, published by Seren, 1992.

Timothy Rees, 'God is Love, let heav'n adore him', published by Mowbray, an imprint of Continuum.

Kuroda Saburo, 'I Am Completely Different', from *Burning Giraffes: Modern Japanese Poetry*, published by Poetry Salzburg, 1996.

Jan Struther, 'Lord of all hopefulness', reprinted with permission.

A. S. J. Tessimond, 'Not Love Perhaps', from the *Collected Works of A. S. J. Tessimond*, published by Whiteknights Press.

R. S. Thomas, 'Gift', from *Experimenting with an Amen*, published by Macmillan, 1986.

James Tipton, 'After Years of Listening', from *Letters from a Stranger*, published by Conundrum Press, 1998.

Helen Waddell, 'The Mournes', reprinted with permission.

David Wagoner, 'The Old Words', from *Riverbed* © David Wagoner, reprinted with permission.